SPIRITUAL WHISPERS

Poetry Collection
By
Rochelle Moore

Dedicated
To
RICHARD

3

MIND, BODY & SPIRITUAL
POETRY COLLECTION

by

Rochelle Moore

Rochelle Moore is a self help author with three published books

KARMA - *(spiritual)*
AROMATHERAPY & HERBALISM - *(body)*
WHEN THE LEVEE BREAKS - *(mind)*

Available from www.mandala-press.com or www.amazon.com

Childrens Books with Morals

SNODVARK THE NAUGHTY DRAGON

Available from www.amazon.com

Poetry

*Published in various books, magazines, online,
won competitions in the UK & USA*
SPIRITUAL WHISPERS
featured in
The Many Hues of Life
The Power of Poetry
Dappled Dreamscapes
Changing Seasons

Rochelle is also a freelance writer

5

6

SPIRITUAL WHISPERS

SPRING

SPRINGTIME

Spring, air so fresh and sweet
Pretty flowers grow 'neath our feet
Rain falls soft from clouds above
In our hearts we soar with love
No more ice, cold nor snow
Green grass explodes
and all life grows.

DAYBREAK

Daybreak, beauty opens
as night sneaks away
Light clawing back
nocturnal scenes vanish
The sky bleeds its goodbye
As the wispy orb
of the moon
disappears
How many times
has this transpired
without witness?
In silent magic
a new day dawns

TRANQUILITY

Close your eyes and visualise
a place of love and peace.
Hear inside, a river's flow
let go, outside world, cease.

Prisms of vivid colors see
rainbow's arching high.
Bright blue backdrop hovers calm,
a wondrous tranquil sky.

Let the outer world be gone.
Settle down and feel
the colors, peace, tranquility.
Feel it, make it real.

Lay your body down to rest
upon the cool green grass.
Open up your inner eye
in here, no time to pass.

The sound of water flowing.
The wondrous warming Sun.
Settle now your inner soul
relax and be as one.

11

Watch the flitting Butterfly
with enormous colored wings.
Listen to the chorus
of the songbird as it sings.

With inner mind and spirit
relax now to your core.
Your body lies in perfect peace,
visit again, when you need more.

You open up your shiny eyes
and feel so fresh, anew.
Your journey's end has come again.
Awaken, tranquil through.

MOTHER.

12

PERFECTION

Where the mountains
meet the sky
Where clouds
as pure as ice
shall reign
Mist on mountains
is her art
Question her for
your advice
Set forth with hope
forget destain
Never shaken
by the
winds of change

SPRING

Spring explodes with colors true.
Flowers, trees all grow anew.
Dewdrops twinkle, grass so green.
Buds burst open, proudly gleam.
Scent of flowers, magic dreams.
Spiderwebs glisten, misty sheen.

Echoes cry the cuckoo's call.
Sunbeams casting shadows tall.
Sweetly scented air all around.
Grass exploding from the ground.
Bees flit busily, buzzing sound.
Cat naps silently on shady mound.

Rejuvenation, life and serenity
the bliss of Spring I love to see.
Sheer joy at new discoveries
a cloak of rebirth my vision sees.

Across the verdant glade
Beholder to your brilliance
Beneath the zenith of the day
A treasure of moments
The beat of living rings
A melody to me
A pool of joy surrounds
Perfections misty cloak
Revealing the countenance of life

Grandma

PRECIOUS TIME

A priceless commodity.
Doubtless clouds
nourish my spirit.
Now above the concerns
of clocks and schedules.
No longer shackled
to relentless demands.
Sleepless nights
now out of reach.
The warmth of time
frees my spirit.
Precious time.

ANGELS

These spirits work beyond our sight
With wings spread wide they guide with light
Their loving arms embrace our souls
Holding close when life's wind blows cold
Whenever you are lost or down
They guide you towards Heaven's crown
All warmth and rays from the sun above
Will shine through silver clouds with love
The essence of all good that's been
Their physical form to us, unseen.

Midnight

19

Animal Friends

Again the early-morning sun
is generous with it's warmth.
With flowing tail and flying mane,
wide nostrils flared,
bold on rein.
He serves without servility
and fights without enmity.
This noble beast,
so swift, courageous,
no pride nor vanity.
The rhythm of his hooves
carries me on and on.
A silent rebuke,
an outspoken praise,
a part of my home.
But remember,
this creature's alive
and only on loan.
A companion, together,
you take on an adventure of love.
A horse is a treasure
which has been lent to man
from God above.

20

EARTH'S HEARTBEAT

It mirrors my own being
to walk with reverence slowly
among the gentle shadows
I linger for a moment
embracing the new view of morn
Of mother earth awakenings
I smile with gentle gratitude
as earth's heartbeat rebounds in unison.

CANVAS OF LIFE

Nature took a blank canvas
our own universe
With big and bold brushstrokes
our world she did commence
Painting in the outlines
with a lavish flair
Each minute detail
painted with such care
She dabbed in the flowers
and measures tree's height
She switched on the sunshine
and the moonlight at night
Such a wonderful artist
and creator so fine
A painting of pure love
beauty for all time

MIDNIGHT

I take my tack out of the car
and round the stable door.
His large brown eyes and trusting face
peep out to greet, implore.
He whinnies from his stable,
hooves pounding on the floor.
Knowing now its time to play,
to wander and explore.

He knows when I am ailing
and picks up on my mirth.
He nips and dances wildly,
I tighten up his girth.
I sit atop his large gray back
his dapples shining through.
Long white mane with flecks of grey,
full tail flowing true.

As friends we gallop in the wild,
him showing me the way.
Experience this freedom
that melts my blues away.

On return he nudges hard
expecting now his treat.
He watches as wash him down
and pick out his large feet.

I rug him up and turn him free,
out to the pastures green.
I watch his frolics with the herd,
My freedom, friend, my dream.

WINGED MESSENGERS

Illusions sheen longing for all to see
Velvet passing, kissed too delicate to recall
The sky listens to their whispers and their dreams
Fluttering outside of our visionary sight
Winged messengers recite our arrogance
through utterings of ravaged tears.

PRISMED GEMS

Sweet silent jewel at my behest
recalling times beneath the folds.
Remember, silence and attest,
where rivers molten, embarked, the froze.
They daze the eyes in prismed gems
pure diamond carats twinkle free.
Such monuments of era's past
worn on a ring, engagements be.
A vow for all eternity
recalling twinkled history.

SILENCE

Let your conscience sleep and stray
beneath the shadowed dreams and stay
Scents and whisperings all erased
hypnotised within your mortal gaze
Teather of all noises tie
let happiness just flow and rise.
Cobwebbed memories let blossom fair
free the blooms, recall with care.
Mossy remanants of truth's you'll see
recalling memories with duplicity.
Harmony reigns within this place
pure silence brings an air of grace.

BELIEVE

Don't close your eyes to meaning
and see your true light beaming
Don't close your ears to hearing
and hear inner joyous singing
Don't close your heart to purest peace
and feel your everlasting love increase
Open up your heart and mind
and forever happiness you will find

WISDOM

Some say you are born with it
a gift not to be wasted.
Others say it must be earned
savored well and tasted.
Wisdom can't be earned by fools
no matter how they try.
I believe that wisdom's sight
comes from your inner eye.

Born with a gift to treasure
to build, nourish and grow.
Once a weed always a weed
that's Mother Nature's blow.
T'is not confined to humankind
this treasure reaches all.
The secret of inner wisdom
is a sacred and wondrous call.

Remember now your duty
if wisdom you've been granted.
Use it well,
don't waste nor quell,
share with mankind and animal,
this ancient inner knowledge tell
to all who need a warning bell.

INNER LIGHT

May the broken and weary spirit
Lay down unnecessary burdens
Remove all turmoil in hatred's grasp
Strip away anxiety and languishing fears
Hear with ears of willingness and hope
See with eyes of love and fortitude
Walk away from a dark and wounded world
Ignite one single spark warming cold hearts
Rise from the ashes of sorrow and pain
With your inner light a torch of freedom

30

CREATION

Alive, the entire fabric of our existence.
It's entirity breathtaking,
enlightening and nourishing.
Our very essence pulsates
with life, awe and compassion.
A miracle transcended
with ongoing encouragement along our way.
All life grows and seasons thankfully melt
in a collective feeling.
Giving expressions of honesty
and passionate ageless wisdom.
Our inner being outshines
the Sun's own radiant brilliance.
As we stop and thankfully express
our worthwhile existance.
An ongoing miracle thrives
in the togetherness of all nature.

VIXEN

Stealth-like and cunning, stalking her prey,
with military precision she seizes the day.
Willow she dances, enticing you near
seductive and clever, she hunts without fear.
Onwards and upwards she's on a great quest
prey unaware of her temptations test.
Standing four-squared as stiff as a stone
small shivers ripple along her backbone.
She lunges, she fights and off with her prey
with a gourmet night's supper
she's won for today.

THE MORN

The early-morning sun
generous with it's heat
I live with servility
fight without enmity
The rhythm of life
carries me on and on
Nature's treasure has
lent me
the beauty of morn

My Hubby

YOU

YOU touch me
like a sultry Summer's eve
YOU move me
like a shimmering drop of morning dew
YOU love me
in a world devoid of feelings
YOU breathe
therefore, I do

MOTHER NATURE

Mother earth bequeaths
great vistas for the soul.
Speaking with a voice so true
reaching out with arms of pure virtue.
Beckoning forth with silky sounds.
Whispers o're grassy mounds.
Yet none to hold nor none to own
for these great works are her's alone.

MOMENTS

Every moment is a time for celebration
As I navigate the winding path of life
I must chisel my way forward with love
and sing with the larksong above
I scan the infinate universal space
and see within the spark of a distant star
The infinity of life I can now trace
And open my mind's eye to eons afar

36

DREAMS COME TRUE

My dreams are visions
of my mind
I stretch and search
for a better view
I stumble now
upon a prize
and uncovered that
dreams can come true

MOVE FORWARD

Move forward with your life
leave the past behind
For gazing back will do no good
never bringing peace of mind

Leave your shadows in the distance
and follow your new path
Be safe from past illusions
and happiness will last

SPRING RAIN

The frothy rivers
Of cool waters rushing
over rocks and bends
Threading water of thought
Too shallow for wisdom
Seeing the greatness
and power
of uncontrollable depths
Nothing is everything
everything is nothing
The universe is roaring
with spring rain swells
Rejuvenation of earth
where enlightenment dwells.

DOORWAY

The door of Spring
is ajar with wonder
The pathless wood
of immensity
Wide open visage
that twists and turns
Bringing joy in
the knowledge
When one door closes
another opens

ANTHEM OF SPRING

So many anthem's Spring did sing
and contemplated birth did bring
Warmed up the earth with purest light
redefined the darkest longest nights
Now feel the softness and the peace
as Summertime is now released
each season now in perfect place
away now Spring show Summer's face

SPRING'S ADIEU

**Awakening from the
glorious pyre
Spring leaves now
it's heart on fire
Incorruptible light
in it's silence of flight
On a flame shall it climb
towards Summertime**

42

SUMMER

Summer

The plants begin to dress
in amazing colors
Generating life
attracting germination
on the wings of the bees
A warm hand
clasping mine
in companionship
within this season
of rejuvenation
We understand time,
widsom and serenity
as we experience
this season of renewed colors
Our own paradise
sown together
We reap joy
in the promise
of harvest
Our covenant of love
held within this discovery

MY LOVE'S EMBRACE

He softly enwraps me
with deepest care
He secretly possesses
my inner dreams
His kiss is an antidote
to all loneliness
With waves of love
I live entwined in bliss

ESSENCE OF ANGELS

Physical expression of God's very essence.
A rarity captured in minds that remain unaware.
Authentic truth, freedom, courage and beauty.
Eyes that see with acceptance and knowingly care.
Such difference in shape, color and texture.
Each one common and yet each one so unique.
They fly in a mellow flush of rosy light;
As the sun declines o're the mountains height.
Yes! As mortals sleep their peace invades
the human heart.
They melt and blend the rich eventide
of God's blessed Heaven.
Angel's essence abound for all to share.
Wherever your pathway meanders
shall you take God's route?
With the essence of angels
founding regiments along your way.

INNER FIRE

Come bask in wisdom's embers' fire
Let your inner mind relax and glow.
Aflame with ancient knowledge's pyres;
Your destiny not fated, let wise winds blow.
Experience the flame of healing light.
Seek and find a new and better you.
Reforge your mind, block out all deceipt.
Allow this wisdom's glow
to shine right through.

GOLDEN ROSE

My life has been eventful in oh, so many ways.
I try to see the sunshine through all the rainy days.
Once a rose of crimson closed up tightly in bud.
Opened slowly, took a peek,
found it safe to fall in love.

My petals in the sunshine bloomed
so red and fragrant strong.
This radiance kept me open
through years I grew along.

Then the sun just disappeared
and left me in the rain.
I closed myself from this world
promising never to return again.

The loneliness of those winter days
the anguish and the pain
changed my crimson petals gold
and kept me from the rain.

49

A single ray on sunshine shone
recalling happy days.
Then my crimson petals danced
and my fragrance did amaze.

That's when this wonder happened.
Anger, sorrow, all disappeared.
Somehow my buds and petals
have forgiven the hurt of those years.

I now emerge a brand new rose
with petals golden hues;
because I see the sun out there
forgiven, missed and blue.

Dad

SMILE

Your lips curl with an upward tilt,
which makes your nose join in.
A simple smile sets off a riot
your facial changes begin.

Your nose it crinkles slightly,
your cheeks move up a tad.
Laughter lines emerge with glee,
to smile is never bad.

Your eyes they beam like flashlamps,
sometimes can shed a tear.
Your inner beauty radiates
all rigidity disappears.

With a smile fresh features form
appears a brighter you.
Try to never underestimate
just what a smile can do.

So now my worlds that you have read,
erratic though they seem.
Just stop a while and have a smile.
Absorb your inner beam.

BEAUTY

They say beauty is a virtue
in the eye of the beholder lies.
Eclipsing other visuals,
viewed with the outer eyes.
To me it is inner magic.
Emerges for all to see.
With inner eyes you focus
with simple reality.
Beauty is your inner soul,
your spirit, life set free.
A star within, a bright light shines
no room for vanity.
Beauty goes by many names
and mirrors many guises.
From caterpillars to butterflys
at which point does beauty arise?
We are they who give things names,
correct me if I'm wrong.
Be we are not of collective minds,
be different, speak out, be strong.
It's time for all to sit and think
be bold, stand up, ignore.
Collective thinking is good for none.
Beauty, your own meaning explore.

LOVE'S AIRS

The song of love inviting all my passion
The beat and rhythm enticing as I dance
I feel alive and dance with wild abandon
To your every tune I find my life enhanced
Your melodies are sweet music to my ears
Your words a romantic symphony
I listen to your tunes as meaning nears
dancing to the beat of your music without fear.

NEW DAWN

You guide my love to a new height
where the essence of fantasy flows
You bathe my spirit within
your wondrous kiss
A new dawn is breaking
Two souls now joined as love completes
Two spirits wandering
have now found their way
Two hearts beating
as one
as love completes

54

BLUE EYES

**The blue color of your eyes so deep
Haunting I retain the vision through the mist
Your eyes still burn a picture in my mind
My weakness exposed within my inner ties
My recollections dipped in cloudy haze
Amassed is wisdoms fondly velvet kiss**

LOVE'S VISION

Eyes across a crowded room.
Enchanted nights of stars aglow.
Dark red roses sweetly bloom,
rivers bubble, swiftly flow.

Rainbows arc in skies of powder blue.
Electric touches from the one you love.
Beauty radiates in moonlights rays and hues.
Frozen still, doubtless now, true love.

HIS CALL

He called my name softly from his dreams
His voice is gentle as it draws me near
Through open window moonlight brightly streams
I listen to his calling my love I hear
I lie and watch him in worlds so far away
knowing that I will always stay
Life's rugged miles in old age take their toll
United we stand, holding hands,
completing life soulmate's role.

FORGIVE

Forgive me within the self-reflection
of your light
My creator how can I repay this plight?
Despite my recent fall
you show your love
through all the hate.
You won't allow me to resign
even though I crossed the line.
Steering me away
from desperation's cruel fate
You take me back
you whisper
"I't's never too late"
So now my wounds are gaping wide
as you stand steadfast by my side
Healing my inner turmoils
that churn
I offer you
my everlasting love in return.

DREAMS

Dreams are not just fantasy
nor fairytales of your mind
They're color, shape and vivid sounds,
a reality you'll find.
Sometimes it is easier to
forget or just ignore
You see no point, no reason,
to take time to explore.
Your deepest inner being
tries to help you solve
the truth you feel, react,
dispel your worries,
care,resolve.
Focus on the depth of help
within your inner mind
Your dreams recall with patience
and the answers you will find.
Now start you day with beauty
and clean your slate anew
Listen to your inner self,
get up, a new day view.

TRUE CALLING

I can avoid your all
but only for so long
There's that grain of sand
and the hourglass;
and you, I'm drawn toward
I hear you call
and go to you
and hope I can stay the course

PRINCE CHARMIN'

Can you offer a listening ear
to this troubled soul, my dear?
Underestimation in truth I fear
just hearing what you want to hear.

My eyes half-open, can I see?
Your words of love confusing me,
This evil plot and wicked plan
I do not feel it's true my man.

So shake and change I need to do,
this Prince 'charmin' is not for you.
I claimed your word and thought it true.
I burnt with passion and loved you through.

Away on your white horse, go now.
Back whence you came and from my arms.
My heart is melted from all the rows.
Prince 'charmin', no promises
and no more charms.

DESIRE

I long to feel your gentle touch
your eyes they lock with mine.
In hazel-green and icy blue
deadlocked, and lost in time.
Our aura's come together now
and turn a scarlet red.
As lust envelopes all around
all thoughts escape my head.

Your smell is like a toxic scent
that goes right to my head.
My body eager forward pressed
no words need to be said.
I feel your breath upon my neck
and melt beneath your touch.
The pressure has begun to rise
I want you, need your lust.

Our bodies start that dance of love
and slowly, start to fall.
Nothing really matters now no,
nothing else at all.
You claim me like I am your own
and make me feel your need.
I trace my tongue along your lips
with urgency and greed.

No longer can I stand the pace,
no longer, I emplore.
I need my lovers touch to love
want you, like none before.
We slowly lean and freefall down
onto our lovers bed.
I want, I love, I need your touch
plays over in my head.

The pace it quickens swiftly
our rhythm, soft explodes.
My love, I want and need you now
my body lets you know.
We dance the dance of lovers
entwined, embraced, enclosed.
The final moment upon us,
we love, hold and explode.

I lie there quietly in your arms
my love, my world, my own.
I dream of yet another day
when we both return here, home.

SECRET SANCTUARY

Invite me to your hiding place
where all your secrets stay.
I will enter with such quiet grace
explore, and find my way.
I will love and cherish you
and wrap you in my heart.
My promise I now give your soul
our perfect love won't part.

YOUR DANCE

Your melodies are
sweet music
to my
ears.
Your words are
sweet in
romantic symphony.
Your songs of love
inviting all my
passions
to the beat and rhythm
as I dance
to your every note
I am
entranced.

THE WINE OF LOVE

**Love's fragrant wine
which has the sweetest taste.
When uncorked,
releases aromas of deepest red.
Like wine that has
matured for many years,
our love is
savored treasures
not to waste.**

TAKE A CHANCE

I chanced my heart
pursuing more than lust,
Now holding dreams
of true love
my heartfelt dance.
An honest reflection
of happiness
and real romance.
Enkindling bright,
behold my love,
you took a chance.
Now I love you
with devotion
of
immortalized romance.

WEDDING VOW

**My life, the center of my world
Two weddings bands of gold
fused our unison of love.
The words
"I do"
sealed with a
loving kiss.
Souls impacting
now sealed within memories
of pure bliss.**

Kyle

68

MY FLOWER

You are my little buttercup
Glowing as the sun comes up
Beauty, peace, serenity,
your love, with ease,
transmits to me.
I thank you now
for all your grace.
A smile extends
from heart to face.
Birds of love
they sing inside.
Since you became
my ~~kin and bride~~.
Second child

FOREVER

May I always awake
to the wonder of you.
Your soothing voice
a melody of comfort.
Your laughter overshadows
my tears of sorrow.
My heart leaps at your
enfolding embrace.
I give you my today
and all of my tommorrows.

MY LOVE

You know I'm here to understand
When your sorrowful I hold your hand
I'll guide your life and make you see
just put your faith and trust in me
I'll brighten up your tear-stained face
and hold you in a tight embrace
I'll help you hear what others say
my love is pure in a simple way
And when your happy and you smile
it makes me feel it's all worthwhile

SILENT CALL

When called upon I try to do
whatever you request, for you.
With open heart I offer love
as pure and true as a white dove.
Your every wish is my command
you call, I come with outstretched hand.

THE STRENGTH OF LOVE

You show me a mountain
and ask me to climb it
You show me pure moments
of unequaled commitment
You show me myself
as worth of respect
You show me my past
is not set in stone
You show me my future
and hold my being
as I rebuild my heart.

VELVET LIPS

**Velvet lips
like
morning dew.
Kissing deep
like
mystic dreams.
Ruby lips
of
rosy red.
Like buds
hearts open
on
petals fair.**

LOVE NOTES

**Within the hushed light
we are the opening of a book of love
Together in the night
we are one in soul and mind
A melody so sweet
it lingers all night long
The tunes within our hearts
will always play as one**

ROSE BLOOMS

Enshroud in green
sun glossed leaves
Held secret by
the curve of thorn
Enfolding senses
hinting love
Romancing blooms
of scarlet red
of perfect innocence
remade
Proposed to sing
a serenade

SUMMERTIME

Lazy, hazy Summer days
unwind slowly, sun ablaze.
Colored flowers adorn each vase.
Summer's back, your spirits raise.
Sweetly scented all all around.
Grass exploding from the ground.
Bees flitting busily, buzzing sound.
Cat naps quietly on shady mound.
Butterfly angel's colored wings,
zipping merrily, birdsong sings.
Cookoo's call like nature's kings
announcing loudly summer rings.
Lying still while waters flow.
Penetrate deep my inner soul.
Sunshine,silence, tranquility
a cloak of peace my vision sees.
End of day, begins nightfall.
Sun goes down, a blazing ball.
Bats emerge, they shreik and call.
Summer, most beautiful season of all.

SWEET MELODY

Within the hushed light
we are
the opening of
a book of poetry.
Together
in the night
we are one
in soul and mind.
A melody so sweet,
it lingers
all night long.
The tunes within
our hearts
will alway
play as one.

LOVE

My heart leaps at your embrace
Your soothing voice a melody of comfort
Laughter overshadows our tears of sorrow
I give you the best days of my time
Forget the worlds race and stay with me
Always let me wake to the wonder of you

HEARTS

Chiseled by the angels
with a spirit so rare
Luminious treasures
you esquisitely bare
Accepting with fear
my heart volunteers
with innocenct faith
from darkness I appear
Erase all my pain
and I lay my heart bare
I hand you my trust
to accept, if you dare.

80

FALL

FALL

Upon smooth wood
damp fragrance
of the Fall
disrobes Summer
All flora's treasures
burnished bronze
Gentle breezes
turned to churn
The scene unfolds
now rearranged
The scent of Fall
bestirs the onset
of yesterday
The shifting of
the seasons
takes me back
with loving visions
of Summer days

O' TEMPEST WIND'S

O' tempest wind's,
hypnotic flame
Immortal beauty
sings your name
A golden godess
pure devine
Onward march
our Season's time.
O' tempest wind's
billowing breath
Fall departs
to Winter's breath.

MOONBEAMS

Moonbeams prick the darkened skies
disturbing the blackened masss of night
Midnight amplified redressed in noir
Melodic atmospheric tension
Breath stolen by a dazzling moon
Shadows dress and undress the nocturn sky
The night's astonishing playfullness
pushing and shoving for miles.

WAR CRIES

Memories recalled softly
cascading on a stream of real tears
Heart-wounds reopened
renewing fresh pain
of your lost years
Recalling the mourners
as they openly wept
As you left me alone
disbelief inwardly crept
You followed your orders
that I must now accept
War cries
wounds openly raw
Recalling your youth
I sit here
bereft.

THE SORCERESS

No beauty's pride, nor birth, nor power,
no fame, nor wealth, nor age.
Has found a way to change her hour,
with spells she mixes, plays.

Perchance as witching hour us nears
for mankind time to slumber.
Ointment applied, so that she may fly,
through bright starlit skies, outnumbered.

Have o're life each pathways trod
decreed by her own powers.
Amid the silence lone and deep
everwatching mankind as they sleep.

For the spirit world it does rejoice,
noon and night and just one sun.
A magical hour it does alight.
Throughout midnight hour her time's begun.

MAGICIAN

Enchanter, demon, alchemy's pride,
a Magician of wonder forged deep inside.
Betwist two worlds that both intertwine
overlapping, enlaced and completely combined.
Incantations to beings you chant in low breath.
Immortality denied you, for you there's no death.
Accursed your wisdom and your mystic reign
of wizardry's abject within darkest domain.

88

MY HAUNTED SOUL

Subconscious thoughts remain condemmed
buried deep,
within restraints that won't break free.
Admist my heart a pain sealed
with sorrows tears,
unconscious visions roam
within my fears.

Your lifeless eyes
no longer have that spark.
The flame extinguished
by your loyal will.
All life's rules were shredded
like my heart.
To say goodbye,
too hard,
and my heart kills.

POLITICAL WISDOM

A mortal blow dealt
with pleas never heard.
War and torment,
like sheep in a herd.
No wisdom in politics
shall we ever know.
Lost is our trust
as miltary abuse
ever grows.
Enough is enough,
I cry out
"muffled lies".
Governments lurk in
darkness
with false policies.
For if we give up
our rights,
wish to be set free
then where is the truth
in this world's democracy?

LAMENT TO OUR HEROS

Many hearts are left to bleed,
here, at home in USA.
Many souls will not return,
a great loss of life to pay.
Parents, sons and daughters
fighting for the day
that freedom comes to everyman
and terrorism, held at bay.

We lost so many things that day
It's one we'll not forget
Heros came from all around
with all they have, abet.
People from around the world
stood by us at this time.
No human soul with conscience
could understand this crime.

Lamenting all those heros
who's hearts are heavy still.
The valor and their bravery
not let their spirit kill.
To each and all who helped that day
Ground Zero, nation's all,
we thank you for your help and pray
for those who heard our call.

Like tradgies of all terror
from past to evermore
it's time to say out loud and clear
"No never, never more".

We all of us are heros
and all must strive for peace.
Tattoo this saying on your soul
at your peril if ignored,
"Never, never anymore,
dear God, not anymore".

SPIRITUAL WHISPERS

Her lost soul is left behind
roaming shadows of the land.
Her voice whispers quietly in your mind,
echoing her thoughts with outstretched hand.
Touch the windows, feel the frost,
she floats outside in darkened skies.
Feel her presence, so icy-cold
within the confines of your world.
Her mournful sobs and sorrows there,
you see her presence but cannot share.
Light flourescence wisping near
her dew-laden spirit now surrounds.
Memories of a life once tasted,
her tousled hair wildly floats around.
Has it been a thousand years
she roams within this infinate world?
Freed from mortality yet still enchained
her spiritual whispers still unfurl.

DOOR OF LIFE

Bigger than life is choice;
to let pain heal in one decisive moment.
Move forward to a better day;
pull back the blinding veil
and open up the window to your soul.
Remove tear stained scars
with the light of truth.
Move forward to a better day;
a magnificent life,
full of knowledge,
where wisdom's cup
sweet taste of freedom's flavor.
The fullness of your inner being,
now open to teach you
abundance and experience
the complete love of life.

DON'T TAKE MY SUNSHINE AWAY

Don't take the sunshine from my soul
You fill my entire existence
with happiness and joy.
Smooth and keep me safe from
all life's merciless blows
for without your light
grey clouds will reappear
and night's darkness will gather
within me and destroy.
I need your comfort and protection
from this world's cruel attacks.
Don't take your bright and inspiring
glory from my side.
For without you I will be as lifeless
as an Autumn tree.
For your wishful and spiritual light
it the only way
to keep from all the pathways strewn with thorns.

SPIRITUAL FOOD
FOR THOUGHT

Is not the human outlook bleak
must we turn the other cheek?
Is our faith now in the red
all mortal bonds to God, now dead?
For all we know yet cannot prove
life's narrow course we swerve and move.
What use is faith is this new world
when wider paths seem sure, unfurled?
Though all the paths may seem the same
one narrow path puts us to shame.
Behold, through faith, what Heaven sent
Christ, his son's sacrifice sets precident.
No other God can claim this claim
so, chose your path wisely,
and your faith reclaim.

MIDNIGHT MAN

Trumpet the arrival of your being
hidden within the cracks and crevasses
of torment and vacuity
Your silence is deafening allowing breath
no ease when faced with you
Icy cries of aloof disregard
personified, so cold and harsh
I fear the closeness of your hatred
you plant with seeds of anger
Release me from the substance
of your malignity
I long to fly but my wings are
clipped with fear
No face you show,
the warmth in me bled dry
withering with a disturbing calm
I reach towards the sky
beseach forgiveness
and give my last breath
weeping for serenity.

RAIN

The rain falls
o're earth's carpet
disseminating
earthly aromas
My being transforms
intoxicated
as the water
extends deeply
reaching the
roots of life.

NOCTURN

**The moon licks
the sky free
of blue frosting
Upsetting daylight
of complacency
Revealing an ebony
silky black skin
With drops of
portent stars
replacing the day**

FAITH'S PATH

You showed me a hill
and asked me to climb.
You showed me the moments
of pure commitment.
You showed me myself
as worthy of respect.
You showed me love
carefully guiding my mind.
You showed me courage
washing my future bright.
You showed me the past
is not set in stone.
You showed me complete love
and help me to rebuild my love.

AUTUMN GOLD

Golden leaves falling like Mother Nature's tears
One by one, two by two, with great speed
the tempo increases.
Our once dull streets become
paved with hues of gold.
As Autumn's increasing pitch
reaches new heights.
Silently, like the strokes
of an Artist's brush
Golden leaves fall
filling our meadows and streams aglow.
Autumn hues reaching
a wondrous cresendo
For it is time for us to enjoy
Mother Nature's carpet
Too soon comes Winter's chill
leaving naked trees
erect and standing still.

MEMORIES

I retrace my life along a much travelled path
My sight, my scent, my fragment of memories
Within my mind's eys like laden treasure chests
Old snapshots keep passing through my mind
Stills of life held in black and white still fly
I shall hold them so dearly until the day I die

MY GUARDIAN ANGEL

My angel's name is Tarquin
he has some job to do.
To keep my soul on the right track
and giving Hell it's due
His job entails my freedom
the delivery of my soul
To his master high above
and Satan's loss is whole

The count, it is important
for Tarquin, God and Nick
Here's one soul that's not allowed
to fall for Satan's trick
When I get a little lost or stray
from the right path
Poor Tarquin has a job to do
to save from Satan's wrath

I've learned to live with him in tow,
he is a friend, at last
when I reach the promised land,
repose in peace, "it's past"
And reap my hard earned dues now
it's Satan's turn to weep
As I float along in God's pure love
no longer feeling weak.

My new and everlasting life
is totally free from sin
Enternally no more pain nor stress,
Tarquin promised I'd be in
A place of peace and happiness
with no worries anymore
I long to rest my weary head
and wait at God's hall door

My soul flew free at last,
away from all temptation
Nick, God and Tarquin mark-up the count,
I'm not in the equation
So many people left to turn,
back to the righteous path
Tarquin sets off once again
to save from Satan's wrath.

AUTUMN LOVE

**The choices made that changed our life
when we turned towards love's bright light
Now the sweet song of our hearts raise
A duo of love we now sing with praise
No longer empty our spirits know true bliss
Within our Autumn days love's
sealed in one pure kiss.**

LIFE'S PATH

I stumble through the path of life
from mountains high to lonely boggy marsh
Life's path forever twisting up and down
I harvest lessons both serene and harsh
I met you on my journey half way through
United we vowed to complete life's lengthy trip
Life's rugged miles in old age take their toll
Suffice enough to signify nears a six foot hole
Nature's path now gifts us on our trip
We bravely steer our course whatever may
come out way.

ANGER

Volcano of emotions blow
the cap in shattered shards
Purple faced and ranting wild
try hold back your cards
You try to keep a lid on it
this fierce emotion rages
Your inner frame begins to shake
lions released from their cages
Venom spits and voices raised
no sense nor purpose holds
Once released,
this fearsome beast,
let loose, with no control.

ENCHANTRESS

Within the hellish hall
the creature cries
Her heart is wild
her songs and tale remain
I wade amid the waters
of the past
But dare not wade
towards her voice
so damned and vast
Chamed by her magic
drunken by her spell
Cold, beautiful muse
enchantress to the last

YOUR WISH

When called upon I try to do
whatever you request of me
With open heart I offer you
my complete being in serenity
A call of strength
A call of love
A call for peace
compels me near
Your every wish is my command
your loyal servant
with outstretched hand

NEW DAY

Again the early-morning sun
is generous with it's heat
I live life with servility
and fight without enmity
The rhyme of life
carries me
on and on
My life's companion,
together,
we on on the
adventure of love
Nature's treasures
which has been lent
to us both
for this new morn

REVERSE TIME

**If I could turn back time
these words I would unlodge
from deep within my closed heart
I meant to say them more often**

*I Love You
Talk to me
Let me be your guiding light
Let me be your balm in life
Let me shoulder your concerns
Let me be your harbour from life's storms*

What I really meant to say is

I LOVE YOU

MY HEART'S KEY

You enchant the possibilities
of true love
Your intensity connecting
to my heart
Our oneness gifted
from above
Magnetic bonds drawing
from the start
You hae unlocked
my lonely heart
with a key
Who once I was
now who am I to be
I'm now released from
my inner chains
No longer walking
lonely
no more pains

WITCHING HOUR

The bells of hell chime out and toll
echoing throughout the land
Sacrificial screams and snarls
awaken all those undead
Deep within the graveyard
olden spirits start to stir
The wind howls wild
The moon's alight
from the ground the dead arise
Chanting spells of magic
walking on mortal land
As dawn approaches
the curse reverts
Recalling life with dire reproach
re-tracking back the
ground they tread
and return again to
the place of
the dead.

SILKEN TOUCH

Silken touch like
morning dew
Feelings deep
in
mystic eyes
Glowing cheeks
are
rosy red
As heart buds open
like
petals fair

*Kyle as a
baby*

RAVENS

Ravens black
with
sheen of blue,
long beaks,
rock hard,
caw.
Such a rumpus
every morn,
you dictate
our laws.
You come in Spring
to visit,
you stay
all Summer long.
In Autumn
you just disappear.
Fly off,
and all are gone.

ALWAYS *Richard*

I love the way you see
right through my soul
Which glows
like a bright light
when you say
"You love me
just the way I am
and would
change nothing
about my strange ways"
I love the way
I know what's in
your heart
and knowing its
for always
that
we'll never
be apart

ONE MOMENT

Get lost in the moonrays
and let yourself feel
The twilight's beauty
to your soul appeal
Pluck up the courage
and share in these gifts
Absorb in the essence
of nature's own lips

THE SUBWAY

Bullying businessmen barge
through throngs of crowds
Herded, like cattle,
winding their weary way home
Enclosed subway tunnels
add pollution to the air
Ant-like people swarm
in every direction

Thousands, winding
their way home
to their haven
Open the garden gate
finally, time to relax
Forget for one
fleeting moment
the worry of
work commitments

No longer imprisoned
in a clone-like mind
The longing dispersed
to climb inside a shell
Silence reigns at home
whilst bedlam
holds it's loud tongue

Beyond their gate
the key to sanctuary
in hand
Shimmering brass glints
in sunshine fair
Home at last,
the front door
shut firm behind

A few steps forward
reveals the
garden's reward
A stamp-sized haven,
here a man
can refresh
The battlecry
of city life
banished
for a mere moment

WINTER

AN ANGEL'S SONG

A melody I heard today
I never heard before
So sweet, so pure,
not of this earth
it knocked on my front door
Awakened by this glorious tune
a song that I must learn
Mesmorized by airs
of purest grace,
I look,
I twist,
I turn.

For now my eyes
are open wide
she offers me her hand
"Come stand with me
right by my side
and you will understand"
I reach towars this
hushing tune
my hand, she takes, so calm
My feet no longer
touch the ground
I'm no longer
a mortal man

122

I wipe the teardrops
from my eyes
and say my
last goodbye
For now this tune
I must go learn
above the azure skies

HIS WISH

To sin is human by default
What God requires no sin withstands
Rebellious souls wage sin's demise
Every parasite on earth requires a host

God crafted you with an open heart
Pure love is all that He requires
Surrender now, go parasite, depart
Turn back go God and to his desires

IMPERFECT

At first glance I do appear
so deep, aloof
and hold no fear
Full of pride and
full of might
Not a nerve I show
in sight.

But what seems clear
can be untrue
I hide my fears
from all of you
There is a part
that's full of thorns
I harbour from
all of life's storms

MISUNDERSTOOD

Lock me in this prison
Dull my aches and pains
Solemn is my inner soul
my silence all in vein
Dark and deep,
here locked away
A prisoner of despair
Curled up
in a tortured ball
I play with strands of hair
I sit and wonder, why?
Life's dealt me this hard blow
I'm just depressed
I'm not insane
I try to let them know
No ears will listen to my pleads
Nodoby gives a damn
Instead of help and kindly words
alone, no help from man
So many people live their lives
with this living hell
Next time you see a friend in need
please, heed their warning bell.

TIME WAS

My thoughts now drift
in helpless tides
in ghostly,
animated ships.
My eyes,
where secrets
smolder low.
Breathing in
from ancient air.
To close my eyes
and cut
the thread
yet fear the figure
of my dreams.
My cries,
my caution,
screams regret.
Recalling
how
it
'might have been'.

WHERE IS MY ANGEL

I'm searching for an angel
Where lies this love so rare?
Hidden by lack of motivation?
Perhaps ignoring a chance to care
This year is almost over
true signs of Winter's here
Perhaps in hibernation
true love hides in his lair
I search the corners of my world
I'll drink a kiss so sweet
I'll wrap up in a wish of hope
Perhaps, some day we'll meet.

MILITARY PRECISION

The graves of soldiers lie
in regimental lines and unpronounced
Tombstones in long processions
on military parade
Mutness ladens the air
heavily all life denounced
Bundles masses of soldiers
lie cold beside their comerades.
Tears roll down freely
along forlorn faces
Sobering reality,
just to many races
Observing a lone poppy
I concervatively cede
All hearts choke tightly
and weeping they bleed.

THE FLU

Throbbing head, muscles sore.
Chilling cold through you roar
Sweating hot, shivers through.
Body weak, a war in you.
Chattering teeth, freezing feet,
forhead sweats with beads.
Can't lie still, no comfort, heat,
no end of pain, flu feeds.
Erratic dreams full of screams
rock you to your core
No pills that work, you're body beams
and radiates galore.
For seven nights and seven days,
you're helpless, lying still.
One morn awake and try to make
a move, go climb that hill.
You stand with caution, still in fear.
This viral war still rages.
Wobble slow, the end if near.
Begin to turn the pages.

INJUSTICE

I have come to the conclusion, I fear
Although it does not bring me cheer
We have a scourge amoung our land
It's time for women to take a firm stand
Men still walk along, around so free
Strutting proud for all too see
Still today all women still must right
for equality, in payment, that is our right
Men whine if they are treated rough
The more they get, still not enough
We women work the same as men
The injustice here I have to pen
I have thought of a solution, my friends
To put an end to this sad trend
It's time for women to take up arms again
and all unite, take on these men
I can hear the naysayers whispering now
Oh, this treatment of men we can't allow
I fear that my message you just will not see
and with my own thoughts that you won't agree
Once victims, left to all men's fate
Our sisters fought for equality and it felt great
Equality must be restored for all our goods
So, come on now girls, join the sisterhood.

Will

LOSS

I stand before your marbled form
so wet with dew and morning rain
In silent sadness I stand in pain
Too short your days from this earth torn
God's own hand
stretched out for you to go
and swept my love,
replaced by a gaping hole
I weep now tears
not feigned forsaken grief
My sorrows smolders slowly
but shall never smolder brief

EMERALD ISLE
(Ireland)

A glittering Emerald Isle juts out,
looks like a teddy bear.
The people living on this isle,
all know it, call it Eire.
A little chunk is missing
the back of teddy's head,
taken over by another land
poor Eire, nearly dead.
How can any land or thing
live without a brain?
This little part of teddy's head
has made us all insane.
Many dead, for teddy's head
What's the point? We ask.
There is no answer
'tis so ingrained,
the mold is firmly cast.
So how to help poor teddy
it's taken years to ask.
Even now, his brains spill out,
the sacrificial cow.
They wonder how to fix this,
it's obvious to me.
Just get it back together
ALL live in harmony.

GREED

To grip and grasp for gluttony
is a ghastly gruesome game.
Grief and graft for grubby goal,
and ghoulish ghostly gains.

Greatness is a Godsend,
greed's glitter lets you down.
Glowing, gainly, gilted gifts
glorifying a golden crown.

Get a grip and grab a grasp,
go generate some good.
Greed groups you in a grotesque group
Get out and gather fast.

Growing gently, gone is greed.
Gratifying your soul.
Gleefully, growth sets you free
galvanising your new role.

MELTDOWN

Slumping body, tired mind
nothing matters, out of time
Wayward thinking, focus none
where has the real me gone?
Shattered feelings, lost in space
Leave reality behind, it has no place
No more energy to give a damn
Sure what's the point? I'm just a man.
To try to tell just how you feel
to those around, it's not that real
You have to experience this pain
first hand, the only way to explain.
Just rest a while and take your time
The inner you search for and find
You're just worn out, stepped off the wheel
peace of mind is all you need.
Like a broken limb it takes time to heal
so does your mind need space to feel
So rest awhile, relax, let go
and you'll soon be back in life's own flow.

135

PRICELESS

You are my single star
on a cloudy night
Life is nothing
without the love
of another.
You divide my grief
and to me
you are sacred.
There is always room
in my heart
for your fears.
I will stay
when the rest of the
world departs.
My love, our special love,
has unlimited worth.

WE DID IT

Congratulations girls we are a success
Accepted in a world of greed and access
We're wide awake and nobody's fools
With agression and drive that borders on curel

Equality is a brave act to endorse
Lost femininity not par for the course
Just to have a close look at what life's become
A war of the sexes we now all have won

We broke down the barrier that men held for years
Loosening our death-grip by confronting our fears
What's happened to the truth, once born with pride
Where is the mystery we once held inside?

Corporate now is part of our life
No longer clositered, like a precious pearl
The sting of rejection cuts deep like a knife
Femininity now gone our new roles unfurl

PANIC

Like a sly unwanted spy
it slowly starts to bubble
Lurches from your stomach's pit
You know that you're in trouble
Your heart joins in just for the laugh
It beats raise and it pounds
Blood rushes swiftly to your hear
lightness all around

Your ears then think, 'It's our turn now'
and ring like Cathedral bells
Head pounds like a pneumatic drill
it's a living hell
Your body thinks. 'It's fight or flight',
just as your sweatglands pour
From chilling cold to boiling hot
'Stop it', you implore.

Your knees decide they want to play
and wobble too and fro.
Your feet think, 'What a great game',
and root you to the floor.
So there you stand, your only friend
a Brain that says, 'No more'.
Just stop this now with head held high
and make it to the door.

Once outside the cool air flows
into stubborn puffy lungs.
Your brain now gives more orders,
'All get a grip', my chums.
You stand there feeling stupid
not knowing what to do
the rationale of panic
you know not based on truth.

To walk way or go back to
the place where panic found.
Your choices plainly clear to you
to run or stand your ground.
Just how long fo you want to run,
forever and a day?
Or do you have the confidence
to stand up to panic, stay?

Don't let this devil beat you.
Be brave, don't change your way
For if you run,
it jeers and sneers,
for it has won the day.

WINTER MOON

Under the Winter Moon
FOREVER
Let's waltz whilst the breeze
whistles a romantic tune
TOGETHER
Reminiscing of Spring lover's
in Winter's old song
LOVERS
We'll count down each
and ever shortened day
SOULMATES
Enjoy the beckoning of embrace
of yet another season
FOREVER

LOST LOVE

The lonliness of these Winter days
the anguish and the pain
Has changed my inner spirit
now I can feel the rain
My single ray of sunshine's gone
which left me in the cold
I still recall our happier days
memories of purest gold

WINTER SOLSTICE

On this,
the shortest day of all
Make new year's
resolutions
heed it's call
Believe in things
you cannot see
in nature's powers
you must believe
Look for joy
and live your pleasure
View each sunrise
as your own treasure

OH COME
ALL YE FAITHFUL

O come ye to me holy men
now face the judgement from on high
The power you owned I now retake
As Lord, Creator, you can't deny
These wars you make for ego's sake
sins you hide within a secret place
Please bow your heads and take your leave
your deeds have fouled the air we breathe
Just let the rest of good men grieve
heed my warning, you can't deceive
No hyprocrites can hide from me
as shame is written freely
on your false souls
You falsified my holy words,
so bold
You placed imposters deep within
Remember now a warning I tell
Before the peel
of the final tolling bell

YULETIME

Seasons Greetings, merry be
T'is time for friends and family
Wrap up gifts and shopping for
dinner, pressies and so much more.
I ask you just to stop a while
just what is this season all about?
"Have you done,
seen,
or half-done what he seeks?".
Where does your soul go
when it has lost
the concept of the Creator?

THANKSGIVING

Thank you for the gift of family
we know we're not alone
Thank you for the gift of friends
whose paths have crossed our own
Thank you for the gift of life
which, like a sunlights ray
Beams bright, we share our gratitude
on this Thanksgiving day.

FREE MY SPIRIT

When I die, don't bury me
No box of pine I want interred
Scatter me in Nature's air
My spirit free, I would prefer.

I will ascend to my plateau of peace
Not a lonely, eerie, mournful place
No tears must pass your eyes, don't cry
For nobody knows what beyond there lies

I shall return on the wings of a breeze
I will call to you in the rustle of the trees
Across the fields where poppies grow
My soul and essence shall enternally patrol

Next time we meet, I know not where
T'is a mystery I cannot understand
But be assured that I'll be there
My friends, my family, I'm always at hand

TO GOBBLE OR
NOT TO GOBBLE

(Written by a Turkey)

I often think that all the odds
are not stacked in my favor.
The humans who are feeding me
they seem to like my flavor.
So cruel of them to sacrifice
a turkey such as me.
When all I do is strutt my stuff
causing no calamity.
In fact I've come quite fond of them
and they seem fond of me.
For armed with food for the last month
I'm stuffed from morn till tea.
I flinch as Christmas edges near
and gobble at the thought
these humans trying to outsmart me
firstly, I must be caught.
Hide-and-seek is my forte
that, they don't understand.
On Christmas Eve I'll fly away
off to another land.
With not much time to rearrange
a new birdie for the day,
the last laugh shall be all mine
as I gobble far away

CHRISTMAS

No ordinary man is He
who came to us of virgin birth.
To Betlehem out thoughts must turn
where, in a manger he now sleeps.
Sent down from Heaven to this earth
this, our God's own very son.
A sinless Christ who lived as man
a child all Heaven does revere.
Whom shed his blood for all our sakes.
Pray to and sing to God and Christ.
Who is now back home, enthroned on high
waiting for all of us to hear.
For redemption day does draweth near.

CHRISTMAS TREE ANGEL

An angel of a tinsel tree
in longing dreams
she comes to me
A single star
may shine tonight
A gentle lamp
your way will light
Loving as a dream
may be
Angel of a
Christmas tree

150

TRUE PATH TO GOD

Where the mountains meet at the sky
Where clouds as pure as ice shall reign
Wandering, there you wonder why
Shaken by the winds of change
Mist on mountains is His art
Question him please for advice
Set forth with hope, forget destain
Miles to walk with worlds to see
Back to earth
a place to plan
What right path leads
to the Son of Man

Lily

I MADE HER SMILE

My honest love
not blurred with
lies nor guile
I made her happy
brought her
sunshine for a while
I showed my love for her
in so many ways
Forever faithful throughout
all of those
long days
I nurtured her
filled her days
with love and light
The test of time
has left my love
still bright
Her time to leave
farewall my
inspiration and
my friend
My love
a seed has grown
so strong
it's very sad indeed

STAIRWAY TO HEAVEN

I'm walking up to Heaven
on a stairway to the stars
As I climb these golden steps
I near my paraside world afar
Listening to the angel's song
I'm flying with the wind
Looking back towards
the earth
I leave behind my sins

I'm rejoicing with the Lord
my soul and spirit free
Floating on a
large white cloud
o're earth, sky and sea
I'm dancing on
a rainbow
and singing with the doves
For now I have found
true inner peace
in my new home
high above

A TEARS PATH

Tears are shed
from weepy eyes.
Run down
a forlorn face.
Rivulets of warm
wet cries,
along your
pofile race.

They seem to know
which way to flow
and roll down
to your chin.
They drip, they fall,
off anywhere.
A battle you
can't win.

154

They slide and trace
the same old route.
They know it
oh, so well.
These little tiny
rivulets
are very hard
to quell.

Always remember
in these tears so small.
Are tiny little prisms
Rainbows each
they fall

EXTINGUISHED SPIRIT

Amidst my heart a pain
sealed in sorrow's tears
All this life's rules
are shredded
like my heart.
Unconscious visions roam
within my fears.
Your lifeless eyes
no longer have that spark.
Your spirit's flame
extinguished
by His timely will.
I say
"goodbye"
so hard,
my inner spirit kills.

ME

WALK TOWARDS
THE LIGHT

I accept my death without any fear
I am peaceful, scerene
for I know it is near
My heart full of joy,
I cannot complain
Though my life now departs
with a smile and a tear

My heart now sees clear
what my eyes could not see
Renewed with a clarity
for all eternity
A tranquil path walked
as I stroll towards the light
With my arms opened wise,
I'm home, I delight.

NEW YEARS EVE

Enjoy this night and feel all primed
It's part of a ritual cast for all time
Shadow's of yesterdays all disappear
Anticipation of tommorrows filling the air
Gathering together for the New Year
Friendships, bright smiles, a room full of cheer
The clock ticking slowly as the seconds erode
HAPPY NEW YEAR'S
at midnight explodes
Hugs and kisses ignite in all hearts
As the new year commences
the old now departs

HIS LAST FAREWELL

He never heard his last farewell
Now from the heavens he doth view
The silent dash, the ambulance crew
Trying to avoid the rush-hour queue.
Blue lights darting through busy streets
Fighting to revive his life, it fleets
His final journey from his home
His perfect family now left alone.
He sits and rests and views it all
From his new home o're earth, he calls
Those at home they can be seen
Mourful flashes, their tears now stream
Goodbye, my family and my friends
I bid you now, my last farewell.

WELCOME HOME

To sin is human by default
What God requires
no sins withstand
Rebellious souls
wage sin's demise
every parasite
on earth
requires a host
God hand-crafted you
with an open heart
Pure love is all
that he requires
Surrender now,
go parasite,
depart,
Turn home to God
and his simple
desires

DEPARTURE

I've taken so many falls within my life
This souls is new to you to me is old
I look at you and see within your eyes
a passion, fiercely fighting for my soul
You stand there watching as I depart
I know now that I must break your heart
My spirit empty devoid of feelings at all
I run from you towards your freedom's call

REBEL

A tribute to my Dog

I never really said goodbye,
the chance did not arise,
I held your face within my palms,
the light went from your eyes.
My friend forever and a day
you never left my heart.
At twelve you were considered old,
my whole world fell apart.

The day you came into my life,
an oily bundled mess.
I recall the moment vividely
and laughed at you in jest.
I drove you home and washed you clean,
a little jewel appeared.
German Shepherd Husky mix,
I thought you looked so weird.

All through my life you grew with me
in marriage, love, with child.
You knew you were a special friend,
you never left my side.
As time marched on your winter came
so cold and with a snap.
Your ilness stormed up rapidly,
I never got you back.

The Vet told me that you had gone
was time to say goodbye.
I only wish I had the chance before
you left and died.
I saw the light depart your eyes
stood helplessly and cried.
My partner and my confident,
my loyal friend had died.

SECOND CHANCE

A thousand times I've tried to pass it by,
And try a narrow view, no honest eye.
The meaning of these words I won't reveal,
my sight determines that I pass it by.
Unworthy I believe myself to be,
as age creeps up just like a sweeping wind.
My values changed out of my eye espy
the ancient book of truth, I can't deny.
I lived a tarnished life, you understand.
The Bible sits and stares, my mind won't spend
a little time to read it, fill my fare.
My life ebbs slowly onward, I'm aware.
Through years I have dismissed this book of God;
My fear and senses rusted now with age.
I place my hand and with it the book I guide,
and take a second glance at the first page.

SHADES OF DOUBT

Each breath that I draw no longer beclaimed.
With each day I doubt my strength to believe.
What happened to man and where is his quest?
I ponder and query and cannot percieve.

ETERNITY'S GATES

Oaks in the forest
grow ancient and dim
Sleep with the willow
that weaps o're
the stream
Hope of the spirit
bereft of it's place
Open eternity's gates
let my spirit abide
As part of all nature
for all moments in time

HEAVEN'S PROMISE

My soul cries out
for my lost dreams
For every friends
and family
lost to me
When in despair
You come to me
Lifting up my
weary form
You give me solace
In Heaven's promise

167

FOR WHOM
THE BELL TOLLS

CHRISTCHURCH
DUBLIN

The celtic bells of bronze that rings so pure
The clanging sounds of saints and souls
Its plaintive tone filling Dublin's heart
Will ressurect forgotten beauty, so forlorn
With ancient chant and splended sounds
abandoned now to shouts in far off skies
Metallic, loud and chimeful tolls
that drifts with ease through all the souls of men.

THE HAND OF GOD

Every moment is a time for celebration
as I nagivate my winding path of life
I have been chiseled and seasoned
by his own love
And I sing his glory
like a Stradivarius
played by his own hand
I scan the infinate universal space
and within the spark
of a distant star
I see the hand of God

TRUTH

Through the shadow of truth,
a long road awaits.
Truth shines bright,
go follow your faith.
Truth can be found
and trust can still stand
Engraved a pure feeling
truth it demands
Erase all the pain
and lay your heart bare.
Trust in each other
and God will be there.

COURAGE

In this world of sadness
our earth in a mess.
With wars and disasters
and so much distress.
With floods, quakes and drought
starvation and cries;
No sense prevades
we are living all lies.
Think of the sadness
in a world filled with fright
Have courage and hope
that God will unite.

RESOLUTION

Forgive within the
self-reflection of your light.
Oh, precious Father
how do we repay your might?
Despite my recent
fall in faith
you show your love
through all my hate.
Steering me away
from desperation's cruel fate.
My open wounds are gaping wide
you stand steadfast by my side.
Healing inner turmoils churn
my resolution is my faith
in return.

NEW YEARS DAY

A new year's birth gives life
to the morning's dawn
Birth and death
twin-sister and twin brother
Out goes the old year
and freshly grows another
But victory is not
gained by fight
The old leaves quietly
as the new year alights
Fresh hopes and beginnings
now within sight
Turn your back on the old year
and welcome "what might"

Rochelle Moore

Poet, artist, and self help writer Rochelle Moore resides in Ireland.   She has published three self-help books through www.mandala-press.com which are available on www.amazon.com.   KARMA (the spiritual guide), AROMATHERAPY & HERBALISM (the holistic resource guide) and WHEN THE LEVEE BREAKS (dedicated to everyone on a healing journey.

Rochelle has also written childrens books with her most famous being THE ADVENTURES OF SNODVARK - www.amazon.com

Book 1
SNODVARK THE NAUGHTY DRAGON
Book 2
SNODVARK GOES TO SCHOOL

These childrens books are a magical tale about a lost and very naughty baby dragon who gets into all kinds of mischief.   The difference behind her stories is that each one has a moralistic tale;   SNODVARK THE NAUGHTY DRAGON teaches children that it is "OK TO BE DIFFERENT".

Other Resources

Rochelle's work can be found @

WWW.AMAZON.COM
WWW.MANDALA-PRESS.COM
WWW.GATHER.COM
WWW.FANSTORY.COM
WWW.COPPERFIELD REVIEW.COM
WWW.CYNICMAGAZINE.COM
WWW.SECRETATTIC.COM
WWW.FAITHWRITERS.COM
WWW.BARDSANDSAGES.COM
WWW.SALEYPUBLICATIONS.COM
WWW.WOMENTODAY.COM

LOVE
&
LIGHT

177

Printed in the United States
127096LV00008B/14/A